A Note to Parents

DK READERS is a compelling program for beginning readers, designed in conjunction with leading literacy experts, including Dr. Linda Gambrell, Professor of Education at Clemson University. Dr. Gambrell has served as President of the National Reading Conference and the College Reading Association, and has recently been elected to serve as President of the International Reading Association.

Beautiful illustrations and superb full-color photographs combine with engaging, easy-to-read stories to offer a fresh approach to each subject in the series. Each DK READER is guaranteed to capture a child's interest while developing his or her reading skills, general knowledge, and love of reading.

The five levels of DK READERS are aimed at different reading abilities, enabling you to choose the books that are exactly right for your child:

Pre-level 1: Learning to read
Level 1: Beginning to read
Level 2: Beginning to read alone
Level 3: Reading alone
Level 4: Proficient readers

The "normal" age at which a child begins to read can be anywhere from three to eight years old. Adult participation through the lower levels is very helpful for providing encouragement, discussing storylines, and sounding out unfamiliar words.

No matter which level you select, you can be sure that you are helping your child learn to read, then read to learn!

LONDON, NEW YORK, MUNICH,
MELBOURNE, AND DELHI

For Dorling Kindersley
Senior Editor Elizabeth Dowsett
Managing Art Editor Ron Stobbart
Publishing Manager Catherine Saunders
Art Director Lisa Lanzarini
Associate Publisher Simon Beecroft
Category Publisher Alex Allan
Production Editor Marc Staples
Production Controller Rita Sinha

For Lucasfilm
Executive Editor J. W. Rinzler
Art Director Troy Alders
Keeper of the Holocron Leland Chee
Director of Publishing Carol Roeder

Reading Consultant Dr. Linda Gambrell

Designed and edited by Tall Tree Ltd
Designer Darren Jordan
Editor Jon Richards

First published in the United States in 2011
by DK Publishing
375 Hudson Street, New York, New York 10014

11 12 13 14 15   10 9 8 7 6 5 4 3 2 1

177103—11/10

DK books are available at special discounts when purchased in bulk
for sales promotions, premiums, fund-raising, or educational use.
For details, contact:
DK Publishing Special Markets
375 Hudson Street
New York, New York 10014
SpecialSales@dk.com

A catalog record for this book is available
from the Library of Congress.

ISBN: 978-0-7566-7128-0 (Paperback)
ISBN: 978-0-7566-7129-7 (Hardback)

Reproduced by Media Development and Printing Ltd., UK
Printed and bound in China by L.Rex Printing Company Ltd.

Discover more at:
www.dk.com
www.starwars.com

DK READERS

BEGINNING
1
TO READ

STAR WARS
Tatooine Adventures

Clare Hibbert

Come and explore the planet Tatooine (TA-TOO-EEN) and meet the many different creatures that live here.

This dry, desert world is far
away, on the edge of the galaxy.

Two suns keep the planet very hot.

Planet

This is Anakin Skywalker.
He is a slave who
lives on Tatooine.

He belongs to a
junk merchant
called Watto.

Watto

Anakin fixes machines for Watto.

He builds a droid called C-3PO.

C-3PO will be covered in golden metal.

Droid

Anakin lives in
a busy city called
Mos Espa.

Domed roof

Many of the buildings in
Mos Espa have domed roofs.

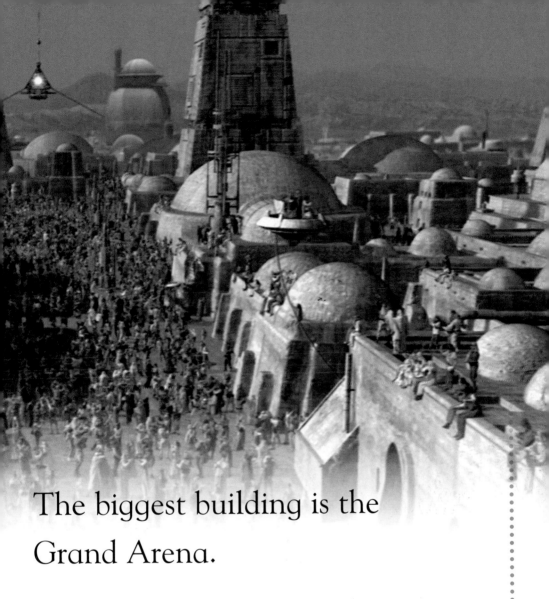

The biggest building is the
Grand Arena.

It has a famous racetrack.

Podracing is the most popular sport on Tatooine.

The Podracers go super-fast.

Anakin is racing. Go, Anakin, go!
Some of the other creatures in the
Podrace cheat, but they can't
beat Anakin!

They live in small camps far out in the desert.

The Sand People are fierce fighters.

Tusken Raiders ride across the sand dunes on big hairy beasts called banthas.

Banthas have shaggy coats
and long, curled horns.

They can survive for weeks
without water.

These little aliens are Jawas.
They are scavengers who buy
and sell things.

Jawas wear hooded brown cloaks.
All you can see are their eyes
that glow orange or yellow.

Scavenger

Wow! Look at this old hunk.
It's called a sandcrawler.

Jawas live inside sandcrawlers.
They drive them across the desert.

They stop to pick up scrap
metal and machine parts to fix
and sell.

The Jawas have found a droid
called R2-D2.

Anakin has a son called Luke.

Luke grows up on Tatooine.

He is raised by the Lars family.

They have a moisture farm.

They collect water from the air.

Owen Lars

The Lars live in
the desert.
The nearest city is
Mos Eisley
(MOSS IZE-LEE).

Moisture farm

Beru Lars

This bar is in Mos Eisley.
It is full of troublemakers.

Luke is here to find someone
to fly him and his friends to
the planet Alderaan.

He asks a pilot
called Han Solo.

Han Solo will
do it.

First he needs
to pay back
some money
he owes to
Jabba the
Hutt.

Is this a giant slug?
No, it's Jabba the Hutt.
He's the most powerful being
on Tatooine.

Jabba is a crime lord.
He loves to make bets and
gamble money.
He has a terrible temper.

Jabba is protected by green-skinned guards.

They are strong, but not very smart.

The guards come from a
planet called Gamorr.
They have horns, tusks,
and short, pig-like snouts.

Look out, C-3PO!
He's behind you!

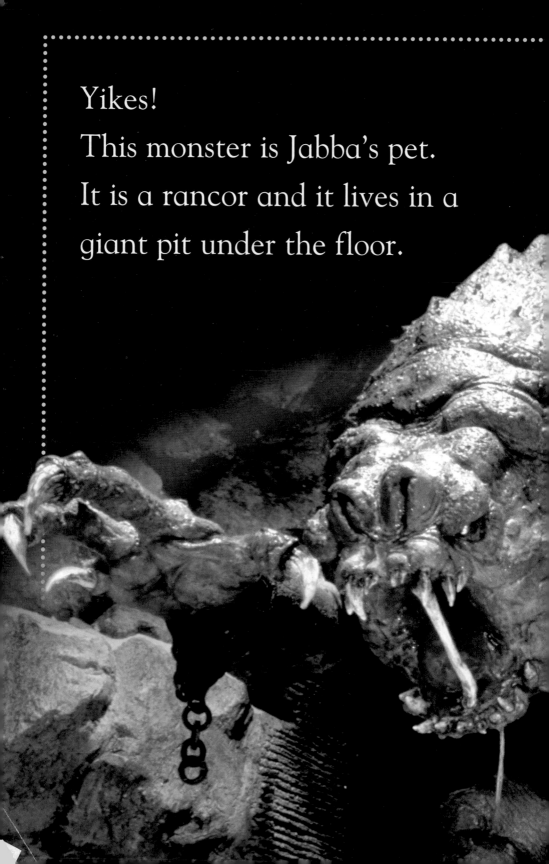

Yikes!
This monster is Jabba's pet.
It is a rancor and it lives in a
giant pit under the floor.

Uh oh!
Sometimes Jabba throws people
into the pit.
The rancor gobbles them up.

Fire! Fire!

Jabba the Hutt's sail barge has
been blasted by a laser cannon.
It's the end for you, Jabba.

You won't be cruising across the planet in this barge again. Looks like it's time for us to leave Tatooine!

Glossary

Droid
a robot

Domed roof
a roof that is shaped like half a ball

Moisture farm
a place where people collect water from the air

Planet
a ball of rock and gas that orbits around a star

Scavenger
someone who collects scrap and bits of metal